A GUIDE TO
RIGHT THINKING
FOR RE-ENTRY

A COMPREHENSIVE STUDY BOOK FOR THE PRESENTLY AND FORMERLY INCARCERATION

BY ANDR'E A. WARD SR.

Published
By
ANDOR Publishing LLC

ISBN NO. 9781726808354

First Edition 2008

ABOUT THE TITLE

One may wonder why I chose to select what seems to be a very specific and narrow focus. However, after having served 16 years in prison and witnessing many people return, I realized there is a serious need for prison officials, criminologists, penologists, community activists, advocates and the incarcerated themselves to re-examine ways to approach dealing with the ***"Thinking"*** of the incarcerated so as to really prepare them for re-entry back into society. Understanding this need then is why I decided to go ahead with the title and focus.

Those of you, who have witnessed my growth throughout the years of my incarceration, know I have assiduously advocated for the empowerment of incarcerated persons. Yet too often, many who have languished for years in the prisons throughout the United States - even the world - have withdrawn their energy and creative ideas from the much-needed work to empower others simply because they are "Tired." However, because of the nearly 65,000 incarcerated in New York State, the almost 2 million incarcerated nationally and a spate of others incarcerated throughout the world, there is no time to submit to the thought of feeling or being tired. Instead, we must all continue to work to effect change.

It is important that history show for all times that those incarcerated have the insights, analysis, and ideas to (in a collaborative effort with communities impacted by crime, organizations, policy makers and prison officials) best solve the problems of recidivism and re-entry. It is my hope then that this work *"**A Guide To Right Thinking:** A Comprehensive Study Book for the Presently and Formerly Incarcerated,"* contributes to this effort.

DEDICATION

This book is first dedicated to the late Edwin "Eddie" Ellis, whose work inspired the writing of this book. It is also dedicated to all incarcerated and formerly incarcerated persons, Prison and Outside Organizations, Faith-Based Communities, Activists, Advocates, and genuine Prison Officials for their sincere effort to address the *"Thinking"* of incarcerated persons by developing innovative, logic modeled, individualized and customized programs that would prepare them for re-entry back into society.

ACKNOWLEDGMENTS

I would like to express my thanks and appreciation to all those who assisted me in completing this work; my mother, Queen Mother Rochelle Archer for her love, patience, support and encouragement; brother Joseph "Doncore" Robinson (Author of "Thinking Outside The Cell: *An Entrepreneur's Guide for the Incarcerated and Formerly Incarcerated''*) for motivating me to write this book; Otisville Correctional Facility Lifer's Reconciliation Workshop Group and especially Reverend Dr. Gloria Askew for giving me the *"INSTRUCTIONS"* to go ahead and create something that will contribute to Re-entry efforts; and Ms. Kathy Rose for unknowingly motivating me.

I would like to give special thanks to my partner and wife, Joheily Gonzalez-Ward and my children Andr'e A. Ward Jr. and Jeany Amara Ward whom I love and honor.

FOREWORD

I f ten years ago, someone had told me that I would today be working in state prisons, I would have replied, "I don't think so," for at the time I would not have been able to imagine anything less appealing to my mind. But now, in 2018, running therapeutic communities in correctional facilities in New York State and a re-entry program in NYC is what I do! No work has ever brought me such satisfaction or so many rewards when it comes to the individuals with whom I work and on whose behalf I act.

The very first time I visited one of our Network communities not far from New York City, I was taken aback by the level of education, intelligence, courtesy, humor and overall decency that I encountered in the fifty-one men present that day. In various prisons over the next few years, I witnessed how those incarcerated persons who show real commitment to the educational and therapeutic programs available "inside" inevitably see the emergence of the promise existing within them since birth, gifts hitherto hidden from the light. I have marveled at the depth and magnitude of this promise buried under and suffocated by the choking layers of poverty, dysfunction, and hopelessness that characterize the backgrounds of so many people in this world behind the walls. What a resource has been lost to our suffering communities! It came as no surprise to me when I recently learned that whereas only approximately 5% of the U.S. population is intellectually gifted, that number rises in our prisons to an astounding 20%! How could this have happened?

Just about everyone who has gone to prison will one day leave prison. All those released go through "re-entry" but not all reach "reintegration" because the barriers and obstacles faced by formerly incarcerated individuals are often insurmountable. Much adjustment is required: to the social system, to conventional norms, to structured employment, to finding ways to organize and live a functional life, and avoiding crime by finding meaning and purpose in everyday existence. Those of us working in the field understand the vital need for the community to contribute to sustaining the efforts made in prison, to celebrate and encourage the enormous transformation that has occurred, and this we do to the best of our ability through the delivery of an array of re-entry services, and, in our case, therapeutic support.

In recent years, a very welcome addition to this endeavor has been the appearance of books about incarceration or re-entry written by the real experts: imprisoned or formerly incarcerated people striving to build meaningful lives behind the walls or who are preparing to or have gone through the transitional process. One of these precious and indispensable texts is the one you are holding in your hands. Network member Andre A. Ward, Sr.'s *Guide to Right Thinking for Re-entry* will become, I believe, the book that all returning people will keep tucked inside their pocket.

Everything contained in this book is corroborated by the most recent research which finds that it is above all positive cognitive change and improved perspectives that offer the greatest chance of full reintegration. How you think is everything, and lest you forget that in the hustle and bustle of the "real" world, you can just dip right into the *Guide*, open it at any page, and find something that is bound to help right then and there. Mr. Ward's organization of his wisdom takes a novel form: each section corresponds to a letter of the alphabet, taking us from "A" for "Attitude" through "Z" for "Zest" with an easy-to-remember aphorism at the end of every "teaching." This author's credentials for writing such a book are impeccable. One of those remarkably gifted individuals mentioned above, he has, during his sixteen years in prison, educated himself to a degree worthy of respect. I can think of few individuals who are actually able to devour and understand the most complex readings (he has read all the greatest authors since the beginning of time) and, after that, find a way to share that knowledge with his peers. It is an honest book, for its teachings reflect the way Mr. Ward lives every moment of his own life: thoughtfully, sensibly, courteously, consciously and kindly.

It has been a great privilege to be asked to write this foreword. There is no doubt in my mind that Mr. Ward's book will save many lives in large and small ways. He has my utmost respect and admiration. After reading his book, I am sure he will have yours.

Ann J. Williams
Executive Director
Network Support Services, Inc.

"WHILE HAVING A PLACE TO LIVE AND GETTING A JOB ARE CLEARLY CRITICAL TO AN INMATES SUCCESS IN THE COMMUNITY, SUCH MATTERS ARE MEANINGLESS IF THE INMATE STILL THINKS LIKE A CRIMINAL, LOOKS OUT ONLY FOR HIM OR HERSELF OR IGNORES THE NEEDS OF HIS OR HER FAMILY. SIMPLY PUT, THE PERSON WHO THINKS LIKE A CRIMINAL WILL ACT LIKE A CRIMINAL SOONER OR LATER. IT IS SUCH CRIMINOGENIC ELEMENTS WE NEED TO START DEALING WITH"

-Brian Fisher
FORMER COMMISSIONER
NEW YORK STATE DEPARTMENT OF CORRECTIONS

ATTITUDE

a) A PERSISTENT DISPOSITION TO ACT EITHER, POSITIVELY OR NEGATIVELY TOWARD A PERSON, GROUP, OBJECT, SITUATION OR VALUE.

Whether you're still incarcerated or soon to be released, you must strive to always have the right attitude.
-Andr'e Ward-

Being incarcerated for violating society's laws is an experience in which your life is indicating to you the need for it to change and make better. Therefore, to achieve what your life so rightfully deserves, you must *"Get Your Attitude Right."*

Getting into a gang or one-on-one fights while incarcerated; receiving ticket/infractions and the disciplinary action taken against you; doing all the negative and non-productive things - even doing nothing at all to properly develop your incredibly valuable life; all result from you having the "Wrong Attitude."

Even upon release, your attitude toward yourself, family members, an employer, other people or a probation/parole or other law enforcement officer must be right. This means treating them as you would want to be treated. And even if those mentioned above don't have the right attitude toward you, it is vitally important that YOU maintain the *"RIGHT"* attitude for your overall personal well-being. In so doing, you could avoid being re-arrested and sent back to prison.

QUOTE: *"ATTITUDE DETERMINES ALTITUDE."*

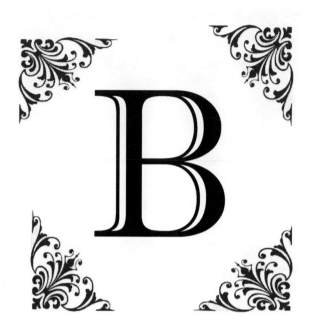

BEHAVIOR

a) THE RESPONSE OF AN INDIVIDUAL GROUP OR SPECIES TO THE WHOLE RANGE OF FACTORS CONSTITUTING ITS ENVIRONMENT.

b) THE MANNER IN WHICH A PERSON BEHAVES IN RESPONSE TO THE ENVIRONMENT THEY ARE IN.

Behavior in accord with the right attitude will ensure your success during and after incarceration
-Andr'e Ward-

Since your behavior (what you say and do) gives others the most helpful clue to finding out who the real you is, it is important that you always strive to behave positively.

Could you imagine that everywhere you went and there were people around, someone was always watching you? And not only were they watching you, but they were doing it when you least suspected it! And could you imagine further that the same person watching you is the very person you're going to meet either to be interviewed for a job or, say, evaluated for how you are progressing probation/parole? Well in these scenarios, how might you behave knowing this? You'd probably positively conduct yourself, knowing that how you behave under that person's watch will determine if your life will be made better or worse, right? So imagine if you behaved positively 99% of the time? You would become one of the most behaviorally attractive people around! This would then bring all sorts of wonderful and positive people and experiences into your life - thus making your life much better.

QUOTE: *"HOW I BEHAVE CREATES THE ROAD I'LL PAVE."*

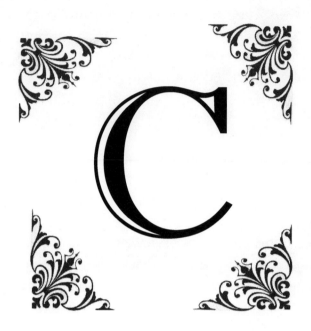

CONSCIOUSNESS

a) THE STATE OF BEING AWAKE AND AWARE OF ONE'S SURROUNDINGS.
b) THE AWARENESS OR PERCEPTION OF SOMETHING BY A PERSON.
c) THE FACT OF AWARENESS BY THE MIND OF ITSELF AND THE WORLD.

To have consciousness one must be aware of themselves and all that affects their life.

-Andr'e Ward-

Being incarcerated or released back into society, you have a unique advantage over those who have never had your experience. You are completely aware of other people's behavior, more than the average person. Even how you see, hear, smell, taste and touch things are different from others and, again, this works to your advantage.

However, after you've spent some time back in society, you lose some of this uniqueness. Why is this so? It is because you are losing some of your *CONSCIOUSNESS*. You have become distracted by the many experiences you are having and are now beginning to *FORGET*. This could prove to be fatal for you because whereas before when you were careful not to do anything that might get you into trouble, you could begin doing things you consider harmless like getting high or being around the wrong people.

Lastly, the very family members and friends you were conscious about while incarcerated, will be made to suffer again if you are incarcerated. And since nobody really likes to suffer, they may not support you anymore as they once did.

QUOTE: *"CONSCIOUSNESS IS THE PRODUCT OF INTELLIGENCE AND EMOTION RIGHTLY USED."*

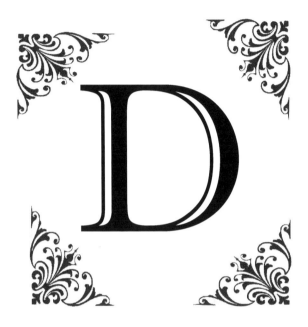

DISCIPLINE

a) AN ORDERLY OR REGULAR PATTERN OF BEHAVIOR.
b) TO IMPOSE ORDER OR MEASURE UPON; BRING INTO ORDER.

Discipline is controlling one's actions when being tempted.
-Andr'e Ward-

Y ou have always understood what it meant to have discipline. You understood this by realizing your favorite basketball player couldn't have become so good was it not for their continuous practice – which is discipline. The Actors, Hip-Hop Artists/Moguls, Entrepreneurs, and Talk Show Hosts whom you admire could never have achieved what they did were it not for their discipline. Even the person that did serve or is serving time with you, who entered prison without a G.E.D., but left/leaves with a Master's Degree, could never have done these things if they did not have Discipline. And finally, the formerly incarcerated person who, against all societal judgments could never have risen to become a morally, intellectually, spiritually and materially successful person was it not for the use of discipline in their lives.

For you to become the best person you can be, whether you are still incarcerated or now released, you must have discipline. Learning to stick with the right course of action even when tempted to do otherwise, will strengthen your discipline and help you avoid unnecessary problems. What will you need to get up every day and go to work on time? *DISCIPLINE*. What must you have to pay your bills on time and avoid being in debt? *DISCIPLINE*. What should you exercise when someone you know offers you to get into something illegal to make more money because you make less money where you work? *DISCIPLINE*. And what will you have to practice when some foolish person attempts to provoke you into becoming violent toward them, thus putting you in a position to possibly be re-arrested and sent back to prison? *DISCIPLINE*. Like patience, you must have discipline.

QUOTE: *"DISCIPLINE IS LIKE A COACH OR TRAINER WHOSE SOLE PURPOSE IS TO HELP CONDITION ME TO WIN."*

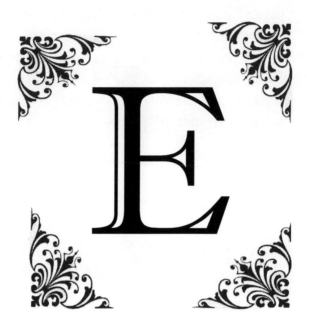

EFFORT

a) THE TOTAL ENERGY EXPENDED AND WORK DONE TO ACHIEVE A PARTICULAR PURPOSE OR RESULT.
b) CONSCIOUS EXERTION OF PHYSICAL OR MENTAL POWER.

Sincere effort is always rewarded
-Andr'e Ward-

H ave you ever seen a baby attempt to stand and take its first step? If so, you witness the incredible amount of effort this little life puts into doing this. Sometimes they fall once, twice and maybe even three times, but by the power of their intense effort, coupled with the assistance of others who watch and eventually begin wanting to help them walk, they finally take that first step!

As a presently incarcerated or soon to be released person, you are almost like that baby taking its first step. In the case of being incarcerated, you should be taking a major step in the direction toward changing the way you think and act. No longer do you want to remain ignorant about your life and what you must do positively to make it better. Nor do you desire to behave in such a way that says to others "I don't care about my life." Instead, you want to become a better person than you were before you were incarcerated.

And not because the Judge told you to do so. Nor because the C.O. or your Counselor said it was necessary. Not even because of your family members or child's Mother/Father or partner said you had to; but because you realize what you will do to change is the best thing for your life and others.

And upon your release, you'll find yourself taking another major step in your life. Faced with fewer restrictions and more responsibility now that you're in society, you'll have to "Show and Prove" to yourself and others that effort you used to change your life (for the better) is now going to pay off. Therefore, by taking steps to change during your incarceration and demonstrating change once released, you'll be surprised how others who watch you will (as in the case with the baby) want to help you become able to do more things on your own.

QUOTE: *"WITHOUT EFFORT THERE IS NO ACCOMPLISHMENT."*

FORESIGHT

a) ACT OF LOOKING FORWARD.
b) ACTION IN REFERENCE TO THE FUTURE.

Foresight is the gift I am given by the Creator to Visualize my future
-Andr'e Ward-

If saying "hindsight is 20/20 vision" means when one has a realization about an event that should have been obvious (for example, Jim realized later that he should not have left his job because he did not have another job to start); and perfect vision and the term "having insight," means one is able to look into one's experiences and completely understand everything about them; then having "FORESIGHT" means planning for an experience you would like to happen in the future.

While incarcerated or even after release, you must possess hindsight, insight, and foresight. Yet, to really accomplish what you'd like in life, you must have *FORESIGHT*.

You may have been sentenced to fifteen, days, months or years; or has only fifteen days or months left before you are released. It doesn't matter how much time you have to deal with, what matters is how you see you're self in the future and what positive actions you will take to become what you see?

There was a person who had been incarcerated at a state prison three different times. In other words, he had committed a crime not once or twice, but three times got caught each time and was sentenced to serve time in an upstate prison three different times.

The combined amount of the time he served was almost twenty years.

During his last stint in prison, which he completed in 1991, his wife reminded him of the time when they were on a visit during his first bid, and he shared with her his vision of inventing a lamp that would clip on to the beach and regular umbrellas.

Well, he obviously did not see it as clearly as he should have during the first time he was not incarcerated, nor even the second time. However, after finally being released from prison in 1991, he went on to invent that lamp and is now a millionaire!

Not only did he see himself creating that lamp during his last bid, but after he was released in 1991, he put what he saw himself doing in the future into action. That is having *FORESIGHT!*

To see yourself learning, growing and changing your life for the better while incarcerated: to see yourself involved in positive experiences and being successful once released, are all clear examples of what it means to have foresight.

QUOTE: *"FORESIGHT IS SEEING WHAT I CAN MAKE HAPPEN IN THE FUTURE, AND PLAN FOR IT."*

GOALS

a) A CONDITION OR STATE TO BE BROUGHT ABOUT
    THROUGH A COURSE OF ACTION.
b) AIM, PURPOSE.

The GOALS That I achieve are only as real as I believe
-Andr'e Ward-

Goals, Goals, Goals. Every motivated person has them. Whether their goal is to get a G.E.D. or Degree; become certified in a trade or even become an Educator, Entrepreneur or a Leader in an organization/company, Goals are absolutely necessary to have to bring out the best of your ability.

Before you being caught and then incarcerated for the crime(s) you committed, your negative actions indicated that you were a highly motivated person. However, that kind of motivation only caused yourself and others to experience grief, pain, and loss.

Yet imagine having goals that could cause you and others to experience Joy, Prosperity, and Happiness. Wouldn't that feel great? No longer motivated by negativity and wrongdoing, your life would now become positive, making your very presence one to be welcomed at any positive gathering. So while incarcerated or even upon release, you must have goals. Some goals may be ones you'd like to accomplish over a short period of time (short-term Goals), while other goals you'd like to achieve over a longer period of time say, a few years, would be your (Long-Term Goals).

QUOTE: *"CREATE POSITIVE GOALS, AND YOUR GOALS WILL POSITIVELY CREATE FOR YOU."*

HUMILITY

a) FREEDOM FROM PRIDE OR ARROGANCE.
b) THE QUALITY OR STATE OF BEING HUMBLE.

Having humility is exercising restraint when facing a challenge because you're confident of your abilities.
-Andr'e Ward-

Having *HUMILITY* during and after incarceration is not easy for most. Recognizing the need to be taught, because you don't know everything; being told that what you want you can't have; and accepting the only available job at the time which pays very little; to endure these three things, you must have *HUMILITY*.

Often times the reason for you getting into trouble was because you lacked humility. You felt that being humble (having humility) meant you were weak, a coward or a pushover. However, did you know that while it's easy to be aggressive, disrespectful and intimidating, it takes real power and strength to exercise humility!

At the age of twenty years old Johnny was known to be the notorious one in the Foster Housing Projects where he grew up. He sold drugs, enforced the rules that governed that lifestyle and even killed. On a Monday evening, while inside of the lobby of the building he lived in, Johnny was arrested and charged with murder, kidnapping, possession of a bulletproof vest and gun. Johnny was in serious trouble. After spending two years going back and forth to the court from Riker's Island, Johnny finally pled guilty to lesser Charge's and was sentenced to serve 15 to 20 years.

Now at Forty-two years old having served 20 years Johnny has finally been released from prison. Yet he is a totally different person from what he once was. While serving his sentence, Johnny went to college, developed himself, spiritually and morally and vowed to himself that as long as he lived, he would never commit a crime nor do wrong.

Yet while Johnny and those who were around him during the twenty years he had done knew he was a completely different person, many people who he began to see, once released,e did not think so.

Johnny was ridiculed by his old crime partners because he told them he no longer was into criminal activity. His old girlfriends whom, he used sexually mocked him because he told them he no longer wanted to mess around with many women and only wanted one. The arresting officers in his case who saw him after his release harassed him by saying he'd always be a criminal. Yet Johnny never once pridefully or arrogantly responded to these situations, he kept his poise, maintained his humility and went on to become successful.

Can you, like Johnny express humility?

QUOTE: *"WHEN ANYONE MAINTAINS HUMILITY, NOT AFTER PRAISE BUT AFTER BLAME, THEN THEIR HUMILITY JS REAL."*

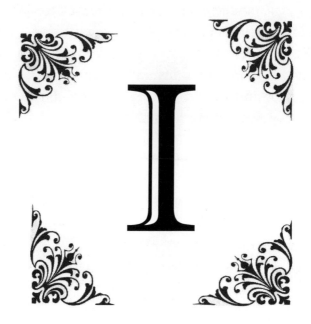

INTEGRITY

(a) UNCOMPROMISING ADHERENCE TO A CODE OF MORAL, ARTISTIC VALUES; UTTER SINCERITY, HONESTY, AND CANDOR. AVOIDANCE OF DECEPTION EXPEDIENCY, ARTIFICIALITY OR SHALLOWNESS OF ANY KIND.

Integrity means being committed in all that one does consistently
-Andr'e Ward-

Y ou've seen those persons with integrity. They are sometimes the least popular yet most reliable person you ever met. They are the people whom you trust with your money and family when you are not around. They're the ones who, if asked to carry out their job responsibilities when the boss isn't around, do so as if the latter were right there. They are the ones who love to do the right thing in all situations because that is the right thing to do, Joheilygonzalez@gmail.com and they care about the less fortunate and suffering and seek to make their conditions better. Finally, they are the ones Co's Prison Guards, Police, Probation/Parole Officers, Family and Community members are the least likely to worry about doing wrong again.

As a presently or formerly incarcerated person, you must have your integrity fully developed. For your entire life, success and peace of mind will depend on it. Be a person of integrity today, and won't compromise the truth tomorrow!

QUOTE: *"MY INTEGRITY IS A REFLECTION OF THE BEST PART OF ME."*

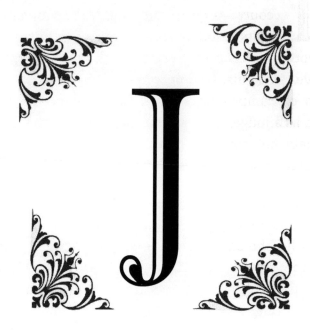

JUDGE

(a) TO FORM A CONCLUSION FROM EVIDENCE.

(b) CRITICAL EVALUATION.

(c) TO FORM AN AUTHORITATIVE OPINION ABOUT; DECIDE THE MERITS OF.

To judge myself first, without being partial, is the greatest gift I can give to myself
-Andr'e Ward-

The Judge who sentenced you during your court proceedings had the incredible responsibility of first weighing all the facts in your case, then determining how much time you'd serve. As a rule, He/She could not be partial, show bias or compromise to satisfy illegal interests. In fact, as a judge, he or she was not only representing society but the very people who are both victims and victimizers (Meaning you).

Imagine if you were a victim of a crime and the Judge sentenced your victimizer too far less time than he/she should have *legally* gotten. You would be the angriest person in the world right? And imagine that you as a person committing a crime went before a judge who would always release you, even when you victimized others over and over again. You'd probably be happy, even though you are contributing to the destruction of society, am I correct?

Well, picture yourself being a victim and victimizer of your own self, during and after you are released from prison simply because of the way you *THINK*. Now in these cases, YOU are your own judge. In the case of the victim then, will you, as the one judging what happened to the victim, judge fairly to satisfy the victim? And as the judge who now has to deal with the victimizer (the negative thoughts which cause you to do wrong), will you sentence the victimizer according to the full letter of the law?

Well when you begin judging your own thoughts and actions like as a judge does when dealing with a case involving a victim/victimizer, then you will greatly prevent yourself from making decisions that can cause you to return back to prison.

QUOTE: *"INSTEAD OF "JUDGE NOT SO YOU SHALL NOT BE JUDGED," IT SHOULD BE "JUDGE SELF SO THE JUDGE DOES NOT HAVE TO EXERCISE JUDGMENT AGAINST YOU."*

That you as a person committing a crime went before a judge, who would always release you, even when you victimized others over and over again. You'd probably be happy, even though you are contributing to the destruction of the society, am I correct?

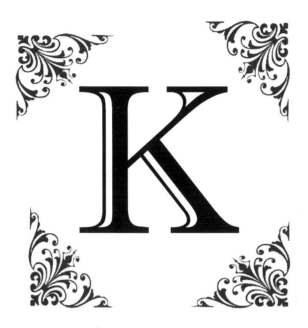

KARMA

(a) THE FORCE GENERATED BY A PERSON'S ACTIONS.

(b) TO FORM A CRITICAL EVALUATION.

What you do comes back to you in like manner
-Andr'e Ward-

Tiffany grew up privileged in the Scarsdale Section of New York. She was seventeen years old and the third child of four, having two older brothers and one younger sister. To others looking from the outside in, it appeared that Tiffany, her father, mother and other siblings were quite happy as a family.

However, little did they know that Tiffany's father was an alcoholic and both verbally and sexually abused her younger sister, mother and even herself. Enduring years of this kind of abuse, Tiffany believed that she and her family were under some kind of "Divine Curse."

After graduating from high school and leaving her parents' home to go off to college, Tiffany thought her life would be better. However, things only got worse for her as she continued to experience being abused by her friends verbally and even encountering sexual abuse from her boyfriend.

Frustrated by the fact that she could not escape this "Divine Curse" she believed herself to be under; she consulted with the one everybody on campus referred to as the "Wise Man." His name was Harold, and he had manicured the lawns of the college for over 30 years.

Tiffany approached Harold and explained to him her past history of being abused at home as well as the present abuse she was experiencing from her peers on campus. Harold looked at her and said "Tiffany, have you ever heard the word *"Karma"* before? Tiffany replied saying that she had but didn't know much about it.

Harold went on to share with Tiffany that while she had no control over what her Father had done to her and her siblings, she did have control over not allowing herself to experience being abused by anyone, any longer. He further explained to Tiffany that much of what she was presently experiencing at school was based on her "attracting" those things to herself because of how she acted. That was the Karma she was creating. Tiffany didn't realize how she actually verbally abused other people by talking to them as though they were beneath her. Nor did she understand that by challenging her boyfriend in very disrespectful ways during their more intimate times, he would end up abusing her sexually. Yet after contemplating what the wise man shared with her, Tiffany decided to change the way she thought about and acted toward others.

It seemed as though instantly all of Tiffany's relationships changed. She began behaving positively toward others; and in turn, others began positively responding to her. In Tiffany's case of

"Karma" then, she began doing things in her life and the lives of others to change her reality.

Now as a presently or soon to be released person, ask yourself *"What kind of Karma do I want to create for myself?"*

QUOTE: *"KARMA IS RECEIVING IN LIFE EXACTLY WHAT YOU GIVE TO IT."*

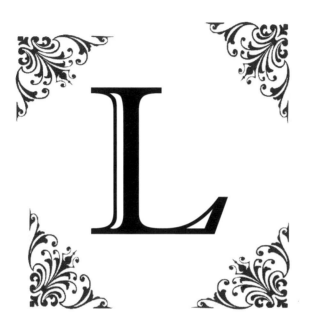

LEADERSHIP

(a) THE ACT OR AN INSTANCE OF LEADING.
(b) A PERSON WHO HAS COMMANDING AUTHORITY OR INFLUENCE.

Leadership is when one's power increases proportionately to
One's ability to serve
-Andre Ward-

I f you found that a country was deviating from the principles upon which it was founded, you wouldn't blame the country itself, but you'd direct your dissatisfaction toward those in positions of "Leadership," right? And what if your favorite basketball, football or sports coach had non-producing players; or the company you've purchased stock from has employees who underperform. Thus, causing you to lose money? You wouldn't be displeased or even angry with the players or employees, you'd probably be upset with the coach, C.E.O. of that company or, in other words, *"The Leadership,"* am I correct again? Well if I am correct about your feelings toward the Leadership in these scenarios, then how you would feel toward yourself if, as a presently or formerly incarcerated person, you deviated from the vow you made to never do things to get into trouble or come back to prison? And how might you feel if you, as the sports players and employees, were non-producing and under- performing? You certainly wouldn't waste time blaming things outside of yourself, would you? Instead, you'd have to blame yourself, isn't that right?

Your own Leadership. You see, Leadership is something you must demonstrate during and after your incarceration. You must be the commanding authority in your life and begin making critical decisions that would positively affect your life as well as society. Hence giving others hope and an example of what true *"LEADERSHIP"* really is.

OUOTE: *"LEADERSHIP'S HARDEST TASK IS NOT JUST TO DO WHAT IS RIGHT, BUT TO KNOW WHAT IS RIGHT."*

MOTIVATION

(a)   DRIVE.
(b)   A MOTIVATING FORCE OR INFLUENCE.
(c)   THE CONDITION OF BEING MOTIVATED.

Motivation is passion in action
-Andr'e Ward-

Important to you becoming successful in your personal development while incarcerated and upon release is your being absolutely convinced that you possess the *MOTIVATION* to accomplish this.

Not one person can make you successful. There is no pill you can take for it. You and only you must possess the strongest motivation to do so yourself.

Everything you see around you exists because of some one's *MOTIVATION.* From the different fashion clothing you admire and would like to wear; the music you enjoy hearing; that house you'd like to own and that college you'd like your children to attend - even this very chapter you're reading now, all of these things came into existence because of Motivation!

Could you imagine a world without motivation? It would be a weird world indeed! Ask yourself then, what can my *MOTIVATION* do to make me a better, more successful person?

QUOTE: *"TO MOTIVATE OTHERS IS GREAT. TO BE MOTIVATED IS GREATER. YET TO POSSESS MOTIVATION IS THE GREATEST."*

NEEDS

(a)   A   PHYSIOLOGICAL   OR   PSYCHOLOGICAL
      REQUIREMENT FOR THE MAINTENANCE OF AN
      ORGANISM.

*What I need can only be gotten when I accept that at the
moment I Cannot go after what I want*
-Andr'e Ward-

Needs and wants, want and needs. These two words you've both said and heard others use repeatedly. Yet, while merely saying these words is quite meaningless, how these words relate to what you *DO* in your life is very, very important.

For example, you know the person who says to themselves "I need to pay my rent with money I've just received from my employer."

However, because someone *WANTS* to buy the latest designer clothing they spend their money on those things and risks being evicted. Then you have the person who *NEEDS* to get a G.E.D while incarcerated but instead, because of *WANTING* to hang out in the yard with others, who also may not have their G.E.D, G.E.D's, never received. And there is yet the other person who knows they need to immediately report to their Parole/Probation Officer. Yet since they want to see their old fling first, does not report and ends up getting violated.

These situations are ones you're sure to be familiar with, either from personal experience or because you know someone who has experienced something like this. With this knowledge then, you as a presently or formerly incarcerated person know better than most that you must be very aware of the difference between what you need and what you want.

Because you have been incarcerated there is the ultimate *NEED* for you to work on the very thinking that caused you to get involved in a criminal lifestyle. You also must positively do any and everything to get programs, assistance, and guidance to aid you in making your transition from prison to society as easy as possible.

Once released, you'll *NEED* to *NETWORK* with family members, friends, and other positive persons. You will also have to be absolutely certain that finding a job, taking care of all your financial responsibilities (i.e., bills, children, special events, and investments) and continuing in the role of a responsible and moral citizen are not things you'd just *"WANT"* to do but definitely *"NEED"* to do.

There is nothing wrong with wanting something like, going on a vacation, taking your children out to the movies, or doing something positive that you feel you deserve to do. However, always remember if what you *WANT* interferes with what you *NEED*, then you must challenge yourself to take care of the *NEED first.*

QUOTE: *"MY NEEDS ARE MANY; MY WANTS ARE FEW; I CAN HAVE THEM BOTH ONLY IF I KNOW WHAT IS MOST IMPORTANT TO DO."*

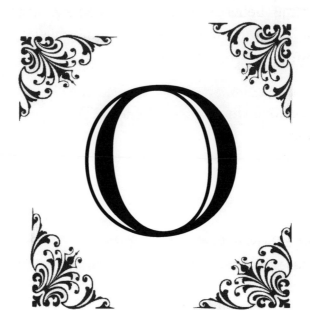

OPTIMISTIC

(a) A CHEERFUL AND HOPEFUL TEMPERAMENT.
(b) AN INCLINATION TO PUT THE MOST FAVORABLE CONSTRUCTION UP ON ACTIONS AND HAPPENINGS.
(c) TO ANTICIPATE THE BEST POSSIBLE OUTCOME.

When someone is optimistic, they consider every failure a stepping stone to success
-Andr'e Ward-

Having experienced or still experiencing being incarcerated, you know there are times when you've faced disappointment, frustration and had setbacks.

Maybe you didn't receive that letter in the mail from a loved one who claimed to have written but failed to once again. Or perhaps after appearing before the parole board commissioners for the third time, you were once again denied release even though you demonstrated having completely transformed your life. Then again you may have found yourself, after being released, having to look for another job only because the one promised to you had been given to someone else.

All of these experiences are indeed ones that are disappointing, frustrating and setback oriented. However, when you are *"OPTIMISTIC"* you respond to each of these experiences in a way that will only allow you to benefit.

And to be optimistic during the many challenges you'll face in life will not only benefit yourself but others too. Without even realizing it at times, your optimism will empower others who have yet to understand what it means to be optimistic. And when this occurs, you will be helping to make better any place you find yourself in, be it in prison, the home or at work.

QUOTE: *"BEING OPTIMISTIC GIVES THE ONE POSSESSING IT INCREDIBLE POWER... IT CAUSES, TO CREATE, STIMULATE, AND MOTIVATE."*

PERSISTENCE

(a) POWER OR CAPACITY OF CONTINUING IN A COURSE IN THE FACE OF DIFFICULTIES.

(b) CONTINUANCE IN SPITE OF OPPOSITION.

Rightly used persistence always gives assistance
-Andr'e Ward-

Nothing of real value is ever given to a human being unless that human being is born into a family that has wealth and riches which are automatically inherited. Everything that someone gains on their own, whether materially or otherwise, comes from not just hard work but *PERSISTENCE*.

Whether you're incarcerated or released, 99% of what you will achieve is largely based on how persistent you have been in achieving it.

It could be something as seemingly insignificant as getting all of your friends to your home every Wednesday to share how they are doing now that they're released from prison; or something as important as letting your love interest know you are very interested in seeing them again and you'd like for the relationship to become permanent. It doesn't matter at all. What does matter is you were persistent at what you wanted to do.

A person that was serving 10 years was finally released in 2005. Having come to prison in his teens, he became certain after spending a decade in prison, that such a place he'd never return to unless visiting to teach and show others that they could do well on the outside.

So once he was released, he went on his first job interview. Believing that he'd be hired on the spot because of the skills acquired over time. He was quite confident. However, much to his dismay he was turned down.

This pattern of being turned down continued. And when he added up the entire job interviews he'd been to and was told he couldn't get the job, it totaled 53 interviews! Yet he didn't give up after all these interviews because for one, he didn't want to return to a life of crime; and two, too *PERSISTENT* to settle for not working at all.

After 53 interviews his persistence finally paid off He was hired at a local McDonald's to begin working as a Janitor. Though the pay wasn't much, he knew with persistence he would eventually find a job that not only paid more but was compatible with HIV/AIDS counseling skills he had acquired while in prison.

****

The year is now 2008. And this person who went to over 50 job interviews and was turned down is now the Coordinator of a program that provides services for thousands of Incarcerated Persons. He comes back into prisons to share what the program he coordinates is about and how he is able to live without breaking the law. And when asked what was it that got him to the point of being the coordinator of such a respected program, his response was simply one-word *"PERSISTENCE."*

The question is how persistent you will be in getting what you need to help you develop and become successful while in prison and once released?

QUOTE: *"PERSISTENCE RESISTS COMPLACENCE."*

QUESTION

(a) AN ACT OR INSTANCE OF ACTING; INQUIRE.

If you want to know the answer to anything, you must first ask
the right question
-Andr'e Ward-

I magine if we lived in a society where nobody asked questions. It would certainly be a place devoid of anyone who could think? We'd probably be walking around like zombies and find ourselves on the brink of becoming extinct.

However, we are fortunate to live in a world where questioning ourselves and others seem to be as important as breathing. And the world has benefited much from this practice. As a person who is presently or formerly incarcerated, you too can benefit the practice of asking questions. Yet before you begin asking others questions, it is important that you begin questioning yourself. Here are some questions you should consider asking yourself as well as answering.

WHO - AM I?

WHY- AM I HERE?

WHAT - IS MY PURPOSE IN LIFE?

WHERE - DO I SEE MYSELF BEING IN 1, 5 OR 10 YEARS?

HOW- WILL I GET TO WHERE I'D LIKE TO SEE MYSELF IN 5 OR 10 YEARS?

WHEN - _AM I GOING TO BEGIN WORKING ON GETTING TO WHERE I'D LIKE TO SEE MYSELF IN 1, 5 OR 10 YEARS?_

Once you begin asking yourself these questions, then you can begin doing what many presently and some formerly incarcerated persons (either because of fear or pride) don't do - ASK OTHERS QUESTIONS THAT CAN HELP YOU!

QUOTE: _"I KEEP SIX HONEST SERVING PERSONS (THEY TAUGHT ME ALL I KNOW). THEIR NAMES ARE WHAT AND WHY AND WHEN AND HOW AND WHERE AND WHO."_

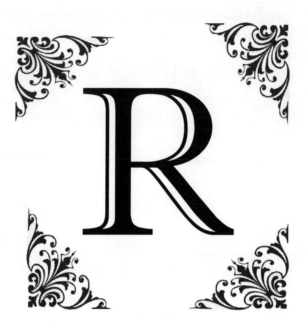

RECIPROCATE

(a) TO GIVE OR TAKE MUTUALLY.
(b) TO MAKE A RETURN FOR SOMETHING GIVEN OR DONE.

To reciprocate should not only mean we should do good things "FOR" others who have done good things for us, but it should also mean that we do good things "FOR" others because others have done good things "FOR" us.
-Andr'e Ward-

During your incarceration and upon your release, there will be many persons who offer to assist you to become the community ready person you should be. These persons may include those who are/were incarcerated with you that sacrificed their time and lives to help create programs and positive conditions for you to develop in. They could've been or still are prison staff, probation or parole officers, employers/co-workers, activists, and community and family members. Whatever their role in life and relationship to you is/was, the fact of the matter is, whether you knew it or not, they were/are helping you.

How then, will you show your gratitude to these persons?

In 1990, a woman had been convicted of murdering her physically and sexually abusive husband. She was sentenced to 5 to 15 years in prison.

Never having been incarcerated before, she found herself angry and bitter because she felt that even though she took the law into her own hands, she shouldn't have gotten that much time for defending her life.

Days weeks and months passed as she still harbored these feelings. Until one day during her second year in prison, she noticed a group of women in the yard reading books and talking among themselves. She had been told by persons she associated with that these women was all respected in the prison because they always worked to create programs and projects that would help develop others who were incarcerated with them. One of the programs they created addressed how victims of Domestic Abuse could learn how to heal from their experiences.

Wanting to free herself from the burden of being angry and bitter, the woman signed up for their 8-week Domestic Abuse class. While participating, she learned a great deal about herself and her feelings. She began feeling better and finally let go of her anger and bitterness.

Once released in 1996, she lay in her bed at home and thought about those wonderful women - many of whom would spend the rest of their lives in prison. She remembered how they taught her to become strong, respected, dignified, intelligent and humble. She thought about all those people they introduced her to who worked for agencies that helped incarcerated persons with their re-entry into society. She also thought about how she would *RECIPROCATE* everything these women and persons had done for her.

So in the early part of the year 2000, after graduating from college with a degree in Clinical Social Work and receiving grant money, she opened up a Transitional Housing Center for Domestically Abused and Incarcerated Women. This was her way of being able to reciprocate to others what they'd done for her. In fact, because she was so grateful to those women, she named the Transitional Housing Center after the Victims Program they created which was called "I Will Survive."

When someone positively assists you, always be willing to reciprocate.

QUOTE: *"I RECIPROCATE BECAUSE I APPRECIATE."*

SPIRITUAL

(a) HIGHLY REFINED IN THOUGHT OR FEELING.

To be Spiritual means to strive and become one with self and the world so as to reach a state of complete balance and harmony
-Andr'e Ward-

To be Spiritual does not just involve the mere performance of a ritual but it also serves as a way one can help oneself move closer toward bringing Mind, Spirit, and Body into a complete state of harmony. Perhaps during or after your incarceration, you attended Jewish, Christian/Catholic, Muslim or other Religious Services. Then again, maybe you didn't attend any type of formal worship service. However, because of what you'll experience both inside and outside of prison, it is/will be vitally important that you maintain a balanced mind, spirit, and body. This is what it means to not be religious but "Spiritual." Constantly viewing movies with unhealthy content like violence, sex, and death; reading non-mind developing books or magazines and always listening to music or people that are expressing negativity; these are the things that cause the mind to become highly imbalanced and you to not be at peace. For your mind is like a muscle that, if not exercised properly, will never grow. Second, your spirit is the essence of your very being. It is powerful yet sensitive. It picks up everything that the mind takes in. To balance your spirit, you can go somewhere quiet and meditate. Or maybe even take a walk to a place that is surrounded by nature - trees, birds, grass, and water. When surrounded by these things (and not a lot of noise) the spirit can achieve its state of balance, causing you to grow to become even more peaceful. Lastly, the body you have is the most uniquely created structure you'll ever know. Each of its systems works together to help sustain YOU! However, just like a high priced automobile, if it is not maintained and up kept, meaning not given the right food, exercised or allowed the proper rest. Eventually, it will break down (you'll have an untimely death).

So be sure to treat your body right, eat as healthy as possible, exercise and get enough rest. It is a fact that while incarcerated or released it can be stressful, so to combat s tress you must maintain a healthy body. When your mind, spirit, and body are working toward becoming balanced, then you are on the road to becoming *SPIRITUAL.*

QUOTE: *"TO BE SPIRITUAL MEANS THE ANCIENT AND ABIDING QUEST FOR CONNECTEDNESS WITH SOMETHING LARGER AND MORE TRUSTWORTHY THAN OUR EGOS. IT IS CONNECTING WITH OUR OWN SOULS, WITH ONE ANOTHER, WITH THE WORLDS OF HISTORY, WITH THE INDIVISIBLE WINDS OF SPIRIT, WITH THE MYSTERY OF BEING ALIVE."*

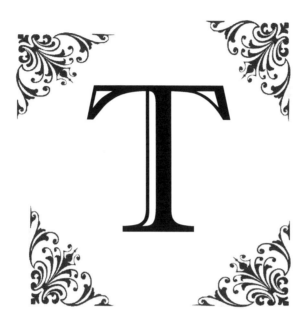

TIME

(a) THE MEASURED OR MEASURABLE PERIOD DURING
     WHICH AN ACTION, PROCESSOR CONDITION EXISTS
     OR CONTINUES.

Time bears patience with no person
-Andr'e Ward-

I f nobody is more keenly aware of what is called time, it is you. Having to either serve time or finally completing the time you had to serve, you understand during your incarceration how crucial it was to be aware of what we call *"TIME."*

Yet while you are concerned about time in ways like whether it was 3:00 or 4:00 pm, or how much *TIME*, in terms of days, weeks, months and years, you have to do before you're released, what is of utmost importance besides these things is what are you doing/going to do with the time you have?

Here are four things to consider about time, whether you are incarcerated or released:

USING YOUR TIME WISELY:

Since time waits for no one, it is necessary that you spend everyday of your life making it better. If you are incarcerated, this can be done by studying information and participating in programs that can help you once released. Or, once released and working, you can take your legally earned money and travel to different places, purchase things you like and help others. You should also be preparing, before being buried in the earth, to leave something of value behind (i.e., Poems/books you've written, Land, Property, Money, or a Notable Reputation for helping to serve other human beings). In these instances, you will have demonstrated that you used your time wisely.

FINDING THE TIME:

Many people say "I don't have time to do this or time to do that. However, they really never create ways to do some of the things they feel they don't have time to do. While incarcerated, you may say I don't have time to get involved in this program or some other positive activity. But what is hindering you from doing these things?

Is it because you don't want to sacrifice maybe a day of exercising or something else that's less important? Or are you simply making an excuse to avoid committing to something that will require paying more than an average amount of attention to? And what about when you're released? What is it that you feel you won't have any time to do? Could it be not getting your body in shape, going back to school, helping a loved one or attending a social function of some sort? Well if it is any of these things above or something just as important; "find" the time to do it.

TAKING YOUR TIME:

While incarcerated, but especially once you're released, you'll see that people are in a rush and everything seems to be moving fast. People no longer wish to take their time; and with the advancements in Technology, you'll soon experience being almost able to say "Presto" and what you want (with the right amount of money, of course) will appear.

But you should realize that moving fast - as is the unfortunate case for many - is not necessarily good for you. For what you feel may be a plan to get ahead in life may translate into you trying to *"CATCH UP"* to others who have some of the things you'd like to have. However, sometimes playing *"CATCH UP"* could end with you getting *"CAUGHT UP"* in something that could jeopardize your freedom. So be sure that when involving yourself in most things that you *"TAKE YOUR TIME"!*

BEING ON TIME:

Since you're living in a world governed *"BY TIME,"* and have or are *"SERVING TIME,"* then why not strive in all your affairs to begin being *"ON TIME."*

The very act of being on time is something that applies to both the incarcerated and those who have been released. While incarcerated, you should always seek to be on time wherever you may go. If you are going to your program, to a special event, or to even see your counselor, it doesn't matter - *"BE ON TIME"!!!*

"After you're released and working, you'll find that one of the most pleasing things to your employer is that you are always on time. Even your family members and persons with whom you interact with socially or business-wise will grow to deeply admire you because you can be counted on to be on *"TIME."*

Start being on time today and the world you live in that's governed by time will begin to serve you.

QUOTE: *"DO THOU LOVE LIFE? THEN DO NOT WASTE TIME; FOR THAT'S THE STUFF LIFE IS MADE OF."*

UNDERSTANDING

(a)   THE ACT OF COMPREHENDING.
(b)   TO GRASP THE MEANING OF.

Knowledge and wisdom are only good if they can produce
understanding
-Andr'e Ward-

One of the critical things you'll need during your incarceration to help you prepare for release *"UNDERSTANDS."*

Learning more about a particular person or situation so that you can use what you've learned to help you (in the most positive way possible) better relate to and deal with that person/situation is what understanding is all about. Therefore, before you are released, you'll need to have an understanding of the following things:

1. *You have harmed and caused some human being(s) to suffer by "YOUR" own actions.*

2. *You are capable of completely changing your negative ways of thinking/acting, even if those incarcerated with you (and who no doubt have many problems themselves) don't want to.*

3. *Those who oftentimes spend their "HARD EARNED" money, lose much needed rest and sacrifice spending precious time away from their children or other loved ones, just to visit you, send you packages, accept your "COLLECT" phone calls and do other things to "HELP YOU", are under no obligation to do so. Therefore, if they decide to stop helping you, do not get angry.*

4. *When you are released, people you know may respond to you in a very over caring manner (sometimes due to the "NEW EXPERIENCE" of*

you being home and their understanding that you need help). However, as the feeling produced by the "NEW EXPERIENCE" lessons because they are getting used to you being home, you will have to accept no longer being given the same kind of attention.

5. *Parole Officers, employers, and family members may give you a hard time; but if you remain consistent as a positive and productive person, they will no longer be a problem for you.*

Decide today to gain an understanding of everything that affects your life, and you will find life being more comfortable to deal with.

QUOTE: *"THE BRAIN IS LIKE A MUSCLE. WHEN WE THINK WELL, WE FEEL GOOD. UNDERSTANDING IS A KIND OF ECSTASY."*

VERSATILITY

a) CAPABLE OF OR ADAPTED FOR TURNING EASILY FROM ONE TO ANOTHER OF VARIOUS TASKS, FIELDS OF.
b) HAVING A WIDE RANGE OF SKILLS, APTITUDES, OR INTERESTS.

Versatility = positively applied adaptability
-Andr'e Ward-

The activity within the society you've been away from for some time and are soon to be released to have become incredibly fast-paced. From the use of the Internet, Cell Phones, Metro-Cards, and other technological gadgetry, millions of people are made to show their *"VERSATILITY"* each day by developing skills needed to use these things. And just as millions of people have to show their versatility, you too will be put in situations where you'll have to demonstrate your versatility once released.

Some people in their ignorance, refusal to learn, and continued complacency fail to show versatility in situations where it is absolutely needed. Whereas others demonstrate their versatility and find themselves progressing further down the road to success.

Here is a classic example of a situation involving one person showing versatility, while another did not: Pete had worked for 10 years as a Mail Room Clerk in an office building on 39th street. Pete was hired based on a referral his Parole Officer had given to the employer.

Pete worked hard, was on time, and treated others with respect. However, while Pete was liked by the employer, he was unable to show *VERSATILITY,* when he turned down a position paying more money on the basis that he had to go through an (on the job) 8-week Computer Training Course to get it.

Sharon, on the other hand, was unlike Pete. She possessed incredible versatility. While incarcerated, she would be willing to learn and become good at whatever skill she could to become someone an employer would be willing to hire.

After Sharon's release from prison, she visited her Parole Officer who helped her get a job as a Mail Room Clerk at the same office building Pete worked in.

Sharon had only worked on the job for a year, but she advanced to become a supervisor 3 months later because of her *"VERSATILITY"!*

Sharon did not become complacent like Pete. She learned about every position in the Mail Room, took college courses at night to learn more about computer programs and when asked by her employer if she'd volunteer to help in a job area she wasn't familiar with, Sharon did so immediately!!!

Sharon demonstrated her versatility and progressed. Pete did not. Your life can also move progressively forward like Sharon's as long as you demonstrate *VERSATILITY.*

QUOTE: *"VERSATILITY IS AN ASSET IN ANY SOCIETY."*

WEAKNESS

(a) FAULTS AND DEFECTS IN CHARACTER.

Weaknesses, Weaknesses, Weaknesses. Everybody has them; most never overcome them; while others transform them into strengths
-Andr'e Ward-

All too often people are released from prison without taking the time out to address and overcome their *"WEAKNESSES."* They sometimes spend years in prison, becoming "Model Incarcerated Persons" who not only interact respectfully and intelligently with the Prison Administration on behalf of the prison population, but they also create and participate in numerous programs even graduate from college earning different degrees with honors. Yet because they did not deal with their weaknesses, they committed a crime once again when they were released.

During your experience of being incarcerated, you have the perfect opportunity to address and overcome your weaknesses. And it doesn't matter what your weaknesses are; you might be addicted to drugs or sex; have poor self-esteem; are easily angered and become violent; you may be impatient, greedy and highly materialistic; or you're a compulsive liar, overly prideful, vindictive, and egotistical, (just to name a few). If you have the sincere desire to address your weaknesses and are willing to ask your Counselor, Chaplain, Prison Program Officials or persons incarcerated with you or even outside once released, about what programs or self- help groups (Organizations) are available to help you address your weaknesses, then you will find yourself on the road to becoming a transformed person, who has overcome his/her weaknesses and is prepared to return back to society as an asset instead of a liability.

So address your weaknesses today and begin to move with real *STRENGTH* tomorrow!

QUOTE: *"THE GREATEST OF WEAKNESSES IS TO BE CONSCIOUS OF NONE."*

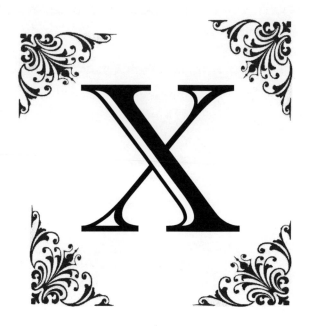

EXCELLENCE

(a) VERY GOOD OF ITS KIND.

(b) OF GREAT WORTH.

To be perfect is an illusion. To strive for excellence can be a reality
-Andr'e Ward-

When taking a serious look at your life while incarcerated, it becomes apparent that your life is not perfect. In the past, you made mistakes, intentionally behaved wrongly and as a result, either offended or harmed others. Some people often remind you of how much you were not perfect, and this can cause you to feel pretty bad about yourself. However, while it is true that you've made poor decisions and intentionally behaved wrongly - thus proving how imperfect you were/are - so has almost each and every other human being - thus proving how flawed they are.

Yet this understanding should not cause you to take pride in the fact that so many (whether they've ever been incarcerated or not) are imperfect like you. Nor should it lead you to now 'justify" the act of intentionally behaving wrongly, which is the worst part of one's imperfection. Instead, you should begin to not be perfect in all you do, but strive for *"EXCELLENCE"* all the days of your life.

Striving for excellence in your life means that you commit to saying and doing nothing less than your (positive) best in every experience you have.

* * * * * * * * * * * * * *

Can you remember a time when you went out to eat at a restaurant and not only was the food good, but those who served you treated you as if you were royalty?

Well, if you did, it's a strong possibility that when asked by someone you know "how was the food and service at that restaurant" your response was "it was excellent"!

And how do you think you were able to receive such excellent food and service? It was because the management more than likely explained to their employees, as you should to yourself, *"Always strive for excellence in all that you do."*

QUOTE: *"EXCELLENCE IS NOT A CHOICE BUT IT IS A WELL ACCEPTED WAY OF STRIVING TO LIVE."*

YIELD

(a) TO FURNISH AS OUTPUT OR AS RETURN OR RESULT
     OF EXPENDED EFFORT.
(b) TO PRODUCE AS A RESULT.

When I invest wisely in any life it "YIELDS" abundance
-Andr'e Ward-

I n the world of finance, every individual investor's primary concern is what will their investment *"YIELD."* Loosely defined, they mean out of the money they initially spent on their investment, how much extra money will be produced for them to receive. When a smart investment is made the investment tends to yield (produce) a reasonable profit. Yet when a poor investment is made, there is a loss of money.

Your life as a presently or formerly incarcerated person is like an investment, and you're the only investor who can determine what it will yield (produce). If you invest wisely in your life while incarcerated or released, that is, you spend your time doing every (positively) possible thing to help better yourself. Then your life will *"YIELD"* a reasonable profit (experiences that will please you).

If, on the other hand, you choose not to invest at all in your life or make poor investments (because you did not analyze them long enough to see how they perform) then you can expect your life to yield (produce) nothing but loss of freedom - incarceration, loss of family/friends or maybe even the loss of your life).

The question is, what kind of investor will you be in your life, will you be one who invests wisely and receives a good yield; or will you be like the poor investor whose investment only yields loss?

QUOTE: *"ONE'S LIFE YIELDS THE VERY THINGS ONE PUTS INTO IT".*

ZEST

(a)   SPIRITED ENJOYMENT.
(b)   AN INVIGORATING QUALITY.

I live my life with ZEST because it deserves the best
-Andr'e Ward-

There are over two million persons incarcerated in the United States, with thousands more either under parole or probationary supervision. Of the many who make up the incarcerated or who are under parole/probationary supervision, *YOU ARE ONE OF THEM!*

As you are/were incarcerated, do know that the American criminal justice system holds almost 2.3 million people in 1,719 state prisons (including New York State prisons), 102 federal prisons, 1,852 juvenile correctional facilities, 3,163 local jails, and 80 Indian Country jails as well as in military prisons, immigration detention facilities, civil commitment centers, state psychiatric hospitals, and prisons in the U.S. territories (Wagner and Sawyer, 2018). Of those 2.3 million people who are released, two thirds (67.8 percent) were rearrested within 3 years (National Institute of Justice, 2005). With the information you've just read, you should understand by now that committing a crime and returning to prison is not an option for you. For there are far too many things you've yet to learn about *YOUR* life; far too many things in life generally, for you to explore and joyfully appreciate; and far too many persons incarcerated who are experiencing constant denials for release at Parole Board Hearings due to the enactment of laws which include *harsher punishments for Non-Violent and Violent Felony Offenders,* for you to make a fatal decision that would have you place yourself back inside of a prison.

* * * * * * * *

It is a known fact that neither life on the inside nor that on the outside is easy. And because you are aware of this, there will certainly be times when you'll find yourself in doubt, experiencing frustration and fear - even anger. However, these feelings aren't just experienced by persons who are/have been incarcerated: at some point in time, all human beings have these experiences. Therefore, what is important when experiencing these feelings is not so much about the feelings themselves, but how you react to them? If you realize that those feelings are temporary, you can move forward in a life filled with

ZEST, knowing that you'll no longer consider being one of the nearly two million incarcerated who never returns back to prison.

QUOTE: "TO HAVE ZEST FOR LIVING IS WHAT LIFE IS ALL ABOUT."

QUESTIONS TO BE USED TO GENERATE GROUP OR INDIVIDUAL DISCUSSION:

1. Which area(s) of the book do you identify with the most (i.e., Behavior, Persistence, and Humility)?

2. What area(s) do you think you need to develop in?

3. Share (specific) ways you can begin working on the areas you need to develop in.

Works Cited

Wagner, P., & Sawyer, W. *"Mass Incarceration: The Whole Pie"*, 2018.

National Institute of Justice: *National Statistics on Recidivism*, 2005.

Made in the USA
Middletown, DE
12 May 2019